20 CLASSICAL THEMES

- Air on the G String
- Ave Maria
- Brahm's Lullaby
- Canon in D
- Dido's Lament
- Eine Kleine Nachtmusik
- Funeral March
- Fur Elise
- Hallelujah from Messiah
- In the Hall of the Mountain King
- Jupiter from the Planets
- Largo
- Ode to Joy
- Pavane
- Pomp and Circumstance
- Sleeping Beauty Waltz
- Spring from the Four Seasons
- The Blue Danube
- The Sorcerer's Apprentice
- Trumpet Voluntary

ARRANGED BY B. C. DOCKERY

Air on the G String

J. S. Bach
arr. B. C. Dockery

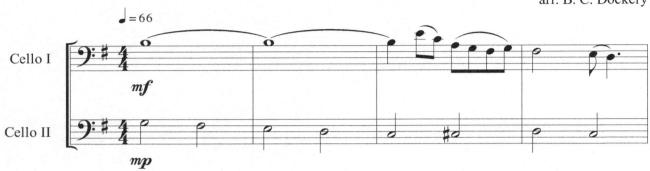

Air on the G String

Air on the G String

Cello I

J. S. Bach
arr. B. C. Dockery

Air on the G String

Cello II

J. S. Bach
arr. B. C. Dockery

Ave Maria

Score

Franz Schubert
B. C. Dockery

Ave Maria

Cello 1

Franz Schubert
B. C. Dockery

Ave Maria

Cello 2

Franz Schubert
B. C. Dockery

Lullaby

Wiegenlied

Score

Johannes Brahms
B. C. Dockery

Lullaby
Wiegenlied

Cello 1

Johannes Brahms
B. C. Dockery

Lullaby

Cello 2

Wiegenlied

Johannes Brahms
B. C. Dockery

Canon in D

Johann Pachelbel
arr. B. C. Dockery

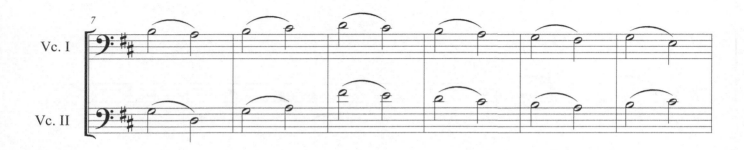

2

Cello I

Canon in D

Johann Pachelbel
arr. B. C. Dockery

Canon in D

Canon in D

Cello II

Johann Pachelbel
arr. B. C. Dockery

Canon in D

Score

Dido's Lament
from Dido and Aeneas

Henry Purcell
B. C. Dockery

©2023

Dido's Lament
from Dido and Aeneas

Henry Purcell
B. C. Dockery

Larghetto ♩ = 56

Dido's Lament
from Dido and Aeneas

Henry Purcell
B. C. Dockery

Larghetto ♩ = 56

rit.

Score

Eine Kleine Nachtmusik

K. 525 First Movement
First Theme

Wolfgang Amadeus Mozart

B. C. Dockery

Eine Kleine Nachtmusik

Cello 1

K. 525 First Movement
First Theme

Wolfgang Amadeus Mozart
B. C. Dockery

Eine Kleine Nachtmusik

K. 525 First Movement
First Theme

Cello 2

Wolfgang Amadeus Mozart
B. C. Dockery

Funeral March

Score

Frederic Chopin
B. C. Dockery

Funeral March

Cello 1

Frederic Chopin

B. C. Dockery

Funeral March

Cello 2

Frederic Chopin
B. C. Dockery

Fur Elise

Score

Beethoven
B. C. Dockery

Fur Elise

Cello 1

Beethoven
B. C. Dockery

Fur Elise

Cello 2

Beethoven
B. C. Dockery

Hallelujah Chorus

From Messiah

Score

George Frederick Handel

B. C. Dockery

Hallelujah Chorus

From Messiah

Cello 1

George Frederick Handel
B. C. Dockery

Hallelujah Chorus
From Messiah

Cello 2

George Frederick Handel
B. C. Dockery

In the Hall of the Mountain King

Score

From Peer Gynt

Edvard Grieg
B. C. Dockery

In the Hall of the Mountain King

Cello 1

From Peer Gynt

Edvard Grieg

B. C. Dockery

In the Hall of the Mountain King

From Peer Gynt

Cello 2

Edvard Grieg
B. C. Dockery

Score

Jupiter
from The Planets

Gustav Holst
B. C. Dockery

Jupiter
from The Planets

Cello 1

Gustav Holst
B. C. Dockery

Jupiter
from The Planets

Cello 2

Gustav Holst
B. C. Dockery

Goin' Home

Largo from New World Symphony

Score

Traditional
Antonin Dvorak
B. C. Dockery

Goin' Home

Goin' Home
Largo from New World Symphony

Cello 1

Traditional
Antonin Dvorak
B. C. Dockery

Goin' Home
Largo from New World Symphony

Cello 2

Traditional
Antonin Dvorak
B. C. Dockery

Ode to Joy
(Joyful, Joyful, We Adore Thee)

Beethoven
arr. B. C. Dockery

Ode to Joy
(Joyful, Joyful, We Adore Thee)

Beethoven
arr. B. C. Dockery

Cello 1

Moderately

Ode to Joy
(Joyful, Joyful, We Adore Thee)

Beethoven
arr. B. C. Dockery

Cello 2

Moderately

Pavane

Score

Gabriel Faure
B. C. Dockery

Pavane

Cello 1

Gabriel Faure

B. C. Dockery

Pavane

Cello 2

Gabriel Faure
B. C. Dockery

Pomp and Circumstance
March No. 1

Edward Elgar
B. C. Dockery

Score

Pomp and Circumstance
March No. 1

Pomp and Circumstance
March No. 1

Edward Elgar
B. C. Dockery

Cello 1

Pomp and Circumstance
March No. 1

Edward Elgar
B. C. Dockery

Cello 2

Sleeping Beauty Waltz

Score

Tchaikovsky
B. C. Dockery

Sleeping Beauty Waltz

Cello 1

Tchaikovsky
B. C. Dockery

Sleeping Beauty Waltz

Cello 2

Tchaikovsky
B. C. Dockery

Spring from the Four Seasons

Antonio Vivaldi
arr. B. C. Dockery

©2021

Spring from the Four Seasons

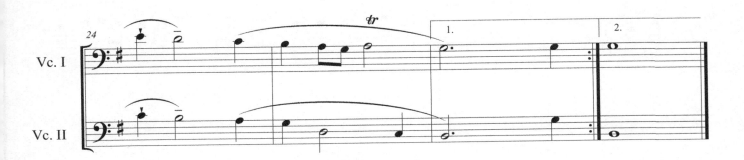

Spring from the Four Seasons

Cello 1

Antonio Vivaldi
arr. B. C. Dockery

Spring from the Four Seasons

Cello 2

Antonio Vivaldi
arr. B. C. Dockery

On the Beautiful Blue Danube

Johann Strauss, Jr.

B. C. Dockery

On the Beautiful Blue Danube

Fine

D.C. al Fine

Cello 1

On the Beautiful Blue Danube

Johann Strauss, Jr.
B. C. Dockery

Cello 2

On the Beautiful Blue Danube

Johann Strauss, Jr.
B. C. Dockery

The Sorcerer's Apprentice

Score

Paul Dukas

B. C. Dockery

The Sorcerer's Apprentice

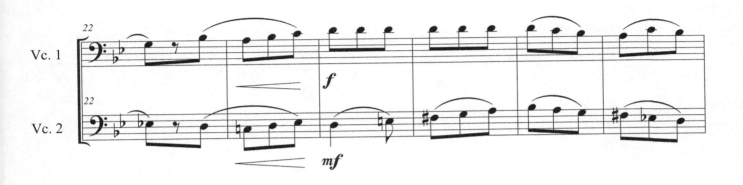

The Sorcerer's Apprentice

Cello 1

Paul Dukas
B. C. Dockery

The Sorcerer's Apprentice

Cello 2

Paul Dukas
B. C. Dockery

Trumpet Voluntary

Jeremy Clark
arr. B. C. Dockery

Trumpet Voluntary

Cello 1

Jeremy Clark
arr. B. C. Dockery

Trumpet Voluntary

Cello 2

Jeremy Clark
arr. B. C. Dockery

Made in the USA
Las Vegas, NV
11 April 2024